Let's
T.A.L.K.:

Your 4-Step Guide To Getting Beyond The Pain Of Loss And The Uncertainty Of Illness So You Can Live Your Best Life Now

Written By:

BeLynda L. Davis

(a.k.a. "Bea")

Foreword Written By:

Elder Steven A. Davis

INSIPIRED2INSPIRE, LLC.

Saint Louis, Missouri

Let's T.A.L.K.: Your 4-Step Guide To Getting Beyond The Pain Of Loss And The Uncertainty Of Illness So You Can Live Your Best Life Now
Published by INSPIRED2INSPIRE, LLC.

DISCLAIMER

This book is intended for informational and inspirational purposes only. Neither the publisher, editor, nor author is engaged in rendering professional advice or services to the individual reader. The ideas, information, exercises, methods, procedures, products, and suggestions contained in this book are not intended as a substitute for consulting with a board-certified physician. All matters regarding the individual reader's health require expert medical advice and supervision. Neither the publisher, editor, nor author shall be liable or responsible for any loss or damage allegedly arising from any idea, information, procedures, and suggestions in this book. Readers are advised to do their own due diligence when it comes to making business decisions and all ideas, information, exercises, methods, procedures, products, and suggestions that have been provided should be independently verified by your own qualified professional. The publisher has used its best endeavors to ensure that the URLs for external websites referred to in this book are correct and active at the time of going to press. However, the publisher and the author have no responsibility for the websites and can make no guarantee that a site will remain live or that the content will remain relevant, decent, or appropriate.

Printed in the United States of America
ISBN-13: 978-1-7369154-1-7
LCCN: 2021907335

For bookings, send your requests to admin@inspired2inspire.co using the subject line *BOOKINGS*. For more information (or if you're a book club, association, organization, or special interest group interested in bulk orders, contact admin@inspired2inspire.co using the subject line *BULK ORDER*).

DEDICATION

None of this would be possible without God's help and grace. I am forever grateful to my family for all their love and support throughout this process. You inspire me each day to live life to the fullest!

ACKNOWLEDGEMENTS

There are a many people who have been instrumental in the publishing of this book, and I am forever grateful for their encouragement and support.

The following list of names, however, are of people who directly contributed to the editing, formatting, publishing, and distribution of this book. I want to use this space to thank each of them for their contribution and service:

Ollie Legette
ChrisShanda Legette
KrisChelle Legette
Randolph Morehead
The Boyd Family
Bishop Anthony Brown & Family
Evangelist Sharon Dardy
Zachary & Carole Higgins
Rene & Mary Neville
Pastor Fowlkes & Kingdom Builders C.O.G.I.C
Living The Word Church
LaTroy & Paulette Fowlkes
Th Ancrum Family
Darnell & Kenyetta Neville

Ronielda Johnson
Robert & Tamala Truss
Niki Kidd & Family
Patricia Leek & Family
Judy Zacharias
Pastor Dawn & Trish Hodges
Shadrea Carter
Lee Davis
Gail Fountain
Tafoya Sutton, Sr.
Adrian & Candice Lesane
New Creation Church of Grovetown
Mario & Lisa Carter
Tomas Fernandez
Terrence Daniels
Pastor Speed & God's House of Faith
Ray & Joyce Sterling
Maurice & Yvette Wilson
Melissa Nocho & Family
Pastor Edward & 1st Lady Linda Ancrum

TABLE OF CONTENTS

DEDICATION...5
ACKNOWLEDGEMENTS 7
FOREWORD..11
INTRODUCTION...21
LET'S T.A.L.K.: TRUST 33
LET'S T.A.L.K.: TRUST REFLECTION QUESTIONS
....45
NOTES: TRUST 49
LET'S T.A.L.K.: ACCEPT 51
LET'S T.A.L.K.: ACCEPT REFLECTION
QUESTIONS 63
NOTES: ACCEPT...67
LET'S T.A.L.K.: LOVE...69
LET'S T.A.L.K.: LOVE REFLECTION QUESTIONS81
NOTES: LOVE 85
LET'S T.A.L.K.: KNOW...87
LET'S T.A.L.K.: KNOW REFLECTION QUESTIONS
....99
NOTES: KNOW..103
LET'S T.A.L.K.: YOUR ACTION PLAN 105
NOTES: YOUR ACTION PLAN 111
RESOURCES & SUPPORT 113
ABOUT THE AUTHOR...117
SPECIAL NOTE: 121

FOREWORD

Life is filled with pain and suffering; that is just a part of the human condition. I can honestly tell you this book's been written by an individual with a "PhD" in life. As the saying goes, "Life comes at you fast," and the author (my lovely wife and the mother of our children) has experienced life coming at her not just extremely fast but also exceedingly hard.

"Bea," as many people affectionately call her, has experienced things that young children should never have to. She has also endured things as a woman that would have killed many other people.

Her story is exceptionally powerful and impactful. What you'll find in the pages of this remarkable book will inspire every reader to face their challenges head-on and tear down those strongholds that prevent their progress. I cannot encourage you in stronger terms to read this book (from beginning to end) because its message will enable you to overcome whatever you're facing.

There is something about the message T.A.L.K. that allows you to release pressure as you express the anger, frustration, and pain that you're experiencing. Talking is the foundation of connecting to God on your way to establishing a strong spiritual relationship. "Bea" has overcome a tremendous amount of pain and suffering, which has helped develop her passion for purpose. This is part of her testimony.

The catalyst for this book is driven by the author's passion for helping others overcome the pain and suffering that often accompany grief, illness, and loss. As the Bible says in Rev 12:11, "And they overcame him by the blood of the Lamb, and by the word of their testimony; and they loved not their lives unto the death," she is truly a walking "sign" and "wonder."

My previous statement will mean so much more to you as you read the following pages because the main point of this book addresses the harsh circumstances each of us must face. We must tackle all life's knockdowns to achieve our destiny. So, we'll answer questions like:

How do you deal?

How do you cope?

Can you make it?

You may be asking God for divine healing following the unexpected or tragic loss of a loved one or from the pain and suffering caused by a chronic illness. In other words, you're requesting God to do something that only He can. You may even have lost an ability that you once took for granted. If any of this resonates with you, it is incumbent upon you to ensure that you read this book all the way to the end. Why? It's going to give you a way out of that pain point you're dealing with right now. It's going to encourage you by instilling hope in your situation that your outcome will be such that you have to give glory to God.

Proverbs 3:5-6 (KJV) says, "Trust in the Lord with all thine heart; and lean not unto thine own understanding. In all thy ways acknowledge him, and he shall direct thy paths." As you journey to a favorable outcome and not one that ends you, this scripture highlights the need to have trust in God. In other words, you need to lean on Him!

Acknowledging God and His power helps you trust and lean on Him because, at the end of the day, He knows everything! Not only is God omniscient and omnipresent, but He's also omnipotent. In other words, He has all power in His hands! When you acknowledge God and allow Him to direct your paths, getting from where you are right now to that expected end is just a matter of time. As you read this book to its end, refuse to allow your frustration, or hurt to cause you to forfeit your deliverance. You, too, can get to that end where you experience God's thoughts of peace and not despair.

God wants you positioned where your testimony (i.e., your story) can then be used to help someone else, and that is exactly what Bea is talking about in this book. I believe her testimony will be of benefit, not just to you but to everyone you love and care about.

Why am I writing this foreword? It's not just because I'm favored to be her husband, but I, too, have had my share of trying times. Although this book isn't about me (that book is coming), I'll share a small portion of my testimony.

I grew up in a primarily single-parent home. As I got older, there was anger and resentment because I didn't know my father well. Consequently, I found myself trying to find surrogates throughout my childhood, whether it was those that were in my family or other male figures at church or school or on my various jobs. I realized (much later in life) that because I had not forgiven my father, I could not receive the instruction or guidance that they tried to provide, even if he meant well.

It wasn't until I decided to give God a try and allow Him to work in and through me that the healing process began. Subsequently, I was able to forgive my father for the feelings of abandonment. This was even more important when I recall the last time that I saw him alive. I was a Company Commander in the United States Army, and there was this overwhelming push to go and visit him in New York, where he lived most of his adult life. Had the unforgiveness and resentment still been in my heart, this visit may have never taken place.

That weekend, we visited him, and he got a chance to meet my family for the first time. He and I were able to share, engage and talk. Also, I was able to release the anger that nearly consumed me. Unfortunately, and to everyone's surprise, about two weeks later, he passed away. I believe God allowed me to have that moment with him on that weekend so I would not be full of regret for the rest of my life.

The reason I share this story is to challenge each (and every) one of you to not allow your current situation to dictate your actions and activities. Trust God regardless and follow this guide outlined by the author.

Many people may not know the story behind my last name, "Davis." The controversy that surrounds my last name adds to the significance of my lineage. I was raised with my mother's maiden name, "Arline," and I did not know that officially (or legally) my last name was "Davis." Knowing and carrying my father's last name is a big part of who I am, not just as a man but as part of my legacy.

Not growing up with my father caused me to have a warped sense of what a man is and should be. Consequently, I was unwilling to listen to or take guidance from the male figures in my life. Instead, I admired those on the street corner.

I learned from watching movies that a man was supposed to be macho and headstrong—one who never showed emotion because that was like a form of sickness. I believed a man should be stoic at all times, without affection or compassion. I never even wanted to cry to avoid any sign of weakness. This caused me to take a long time to mature as a man, resulting in lots of mistakes while growing into the man I am today.

I'm grateful to God and everyone who didn't give up on me. I'm thankful for everyone who was willing to talk to me, who prayed for me. I'm indebted to my mother for laying a foundation of Godly principles that I still live by to this day. I'm also filled with gratitude to the military for shaping my view of the world and opening my heart to be more compassionate. Yes, that's true. Finally, I'm grateful for the T.A.L.K. method you will read about in this book.

As previously mentioned, I've been through my own share of pain and grief. I've had many life experiences and training in leadership. In the area of religious and spiritual instruction, I'm an ordained Elder. I was raised in the church and found out that GOD IS REAL!

God revealed Himself to me, and I trust (and pray) that God will reveal Himself to you as you read on. You'll get to the point where you're able to apply the T.A.L.K. method. It's imperative to talk to God, accept the reality of where you are, receive God's unconditional love for you, and apply that knowledge to become UNSTOPPABLE!

If you're still wondering why you should read this book or what the main point of this book could mean for you, I believe you'll be able to identify where you are, and no matter who you are or what has transpired in your past, God is the Greatest, and He loves you more than you can imagine! He wants you to take Him at His word. He wants you to try Him.

By the end of this book, we want you to have taken a journey to the realization that no matter what you've had to endure throughout your life, with this God-inspired method, you can now turn those terrible tragedies into terrific triumphs. So again, I encourage you to read this book with great focus and intention because it will bless you!

With all sincerity, I'm favored to be Bea's husband and have been blessed to be a first-hand witness to her journey from tragedy to triumph. She has employed the steps you're now privileged to read and has shared a framework that works. I've witnessed Bea as she's lived out each step of T.A.L.K., and she has inspired (and encouraged) me to do the same. As we set the stage for your personal experience of overcoming, I believe this step-by-step guide, along with your openness to God, is going to bless your soul and catapult you to your destiny!

This simple four-letter acronym, T.A.L.K., will inspire and encourage you to conquer your situations. May it cause a shift in your environment and manifest positive outcomes in your life.

So, with that, let's T.A.L.K.!!

INTRODUCTION

Have you ever lost a loved one?

Have you ever tested positive for a disease or an illness?

Have you ever experienced chronic pain and comfort seemed to be out of reach?

If you've answered "YES" to any of the above questions, hope and healing are available to you!

Whether you're grieving the loss of a loved one, fighting for your health, or searching for a balm to ease your suffering, there is an answer!

Chances are, you may already know…

…the Answer is GOD!

There is no way around it. It's NEVER easy losing someone you love. It's never easy battling health issues and pain because they're more complex than many people want to admit.

But God…

God is your answer, your comfort, and your balm in your time of need. Have you heard of Elisabeth Kubler-Ross?

Elisabeth Kubler-Ross is the Swiss-American psychiatrist

credited with developing the "5 Stages of Grief." She believed there are five stages a person goes through when they experience the sudden (or expected) loss of a loved one. These stages are denial, anger, bargaining, depression, and acceptance.

Knowing these stages has helped many people make sense of their loss. But I believe there is no simple idea or one-size-fits-all box to organize the chaotic (and, often, uncontrollable) emotions that come with grief, affliction, and hurt.

I'm glad I know who does…

…and I want you to know Him too!

You may be working your way through school or working to make a better life for yourself and your family and can't seem to find the help you need to make it through. But if you'll just hold on and keep reading, I know the passing of your loved one, or the pain you may feel in your body, or the frustration of having to fight for everything you get is rough, but there is ALWAYS someone you can talk to about the issues you're going through. GOD IS ALWAYS WITH YOU and knows "this too shall pass!"

It's important for you to know that with God, you can do all things through Christ. You can have Him to hold on to and be with you through it all. You ARE never alone. So, depend on God to see you through.

Like many other people, I've seen what loss can do to someone you care about. A friend experienced her father's passing while she was in another state. Unable to visit her family that often, when she got the call that her father had a heart attack, she did not have the money nor the vacation time to travel to see him. Sadly, my friend's father passed away.

She was heartbroken. Not only did she have to deal with the loss of her father alone, but she also struggled with the grief of her loss without family near. It was hard for her to go through it all. But she did! She realized she had pictures to remind her of the memories she made with her father, and of course, she talked to other loved ones (including her mom) on the phone.

My friend also realized she had other friends she could talk to about her loss. Talking it out and sharing her emotions made it easier to get through the many sleepless nights she cried herself to sleep.

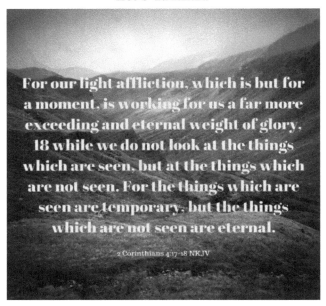

For our light affliction, which is but for a moment, is working for us a far more exceeding and eternal weight of glory, 18 while we do not look at the things which are seen, but at the things which are not seen. For the things which are seen are temporary, but the things which are not seen are eternal.

2 Corinthians 4:17-18 NKJV

I've had my share of hurt and pain. As a woman of God who has lived with Multiple Sclerosis, I've experienced the surprise of a positive diagnosis! I've lived through the pain and overwhelm that, at times, have accompanied my illness. I've also experienced the grief that accompanies the loss of a loved one. Working twice as hard as others, I've fought my way through the aches in my body and the aches in my heart. There were many nights I've thought of my situation and did not fully understand God's plan. But God was always there, never leaving nor forsaking me (Deuteronomy 31:6; Hebrews 13:5)!

This is true for you if you decide to accept this as a fact; more appropriately, accept it as a divine truth!

So, …

LET'S T.A.L.K.

Why Let's T.A.L.K.? Talking about my situation became the turning point for me. Prior to being open about what was going on, I suffered in silence. To make matters worse, I was not one who was comfortable talking as it is. Even in my marriage, my husband and I are opposite from typical couples in that he's the talker (I guess that comes from the preacher in him) and I am soft-spoken and quiet. It takes a while for me to warm up to people but when I do, I'm the easiest and safest person to talk to, just like the girl next door. As I thought through my journey, talking naturally became my slogan and the most impactful way to share and help others in their journey.

You'll be hard-pressed to find someone who has never experienced the loss of a loved one or a loved one who has been diagnosed with a chronic illness.

You may be dealing with a loss, illness, or overwhelming circumstances beyond your control. When you experience any of these situations, just **T.A.L.K.**! T.A.L.K. is an acronym that stands for **Trust**, **Accept**, **Love**, and **Know**.

When God talked, He spoke things into existence. In Romans 4:17, God "called those things that be not as though they were."

After meditating and praying about the grief, hurt, and pain that I've overcome, God revealed this simple plan that helped me get through my lowest (and darkest) moments. Now, I hope it can help you too! It's easy to remember and can be practiced no matter your challenge.

I want to share the steps of T.A.L.K.:

TRUST

When you've experienced life-changing situations and circumstances, it's important to learn to TRUST again. After the tragedy or hurt, you must stay connected to God by faith and remember, "nothing can separate you from the love of God" (Romans 8:39). Once you've learned to trust in God again, you can move on to the next step of T.A.L.K.

ACCEPT

When you're facing life's challenges, it's important to get to the place where you acknowledge them. When you accept your situation or circumstance as real, your healing can begin. God says that His "grace is sufficient" (2 Corinthians 12:9). God has said to me, "And he said unto me, My grace is sufficient for thee: for my strength is made perfect in weakness. Most gladly therefore will I rather glory in my infirmities, that the power of Christ may rest upon me." Your healing begins when you decide you are worthy, and you can move on to the next step of T.A.L.K.

LOVE

God is love, and love conquers all (1 John 4; 1 Corinthians 13)! You can speak the language of love as you continue to talk to your loved ones (even when they are no longer with you physically). If you've lost an ability due to deteriorating health caused by an accident or medical diagnosis, you may feel overwhelmed. Even if you can't find someone who loves you, know God loves you. This will accelerate you to the next step of T.A.L.K.

KNOW

Finally, many have said, "Knowledge is Power!" But, when you apply the knowledge you've gained, that "knowledge" makes you unstoppable! It's necessary that you know you have the POWER to PROGRESS beyond the pain of your present challenge to reach your goals…to reach your destiny!

Everyone's experience is different, but people experience similarities when dealing with loss, grief, and health challenges. I don't know exactly how you feel, but I can share something I know has helped many people cope with losing a loved one.

You might have certain memories of your loved one that can help you T.A.L.K. your way through the loss, the pain, and the hurt!

YOU WILL MAKE IT!

God will never let you down. Just think positive as you're going through life, even during your trials and tribulations, just T.A.L.K. Speak encouraging words to yourself or, as the word says, "speak life" over your situation (Ezekiel 37:4; Proverbs 18:21). You can also sing a song that brings you joy (Isaiah 42:10; Psalms 96:1; Psalms 144:9).

When your loved one becomes a MEMORY, that memory becomes a TREASURE!

AUTHOR UNKNOWN

Have a song in mind and remember that you are not going through your loss and hardship alone. We always have somebody to talk to, and we can T.A.L.K. our way through the hurt and pain. As you're growing and getting through it, you can also have a conversation with your loved one in your heart. Know this is one way to help you get through!

You never have to search for someone to talk to about your trials and tribulations or your issues and situations because God is always there. Release all your grief, pain, and frustration as you T.A.L.K. your way out of your dark moments into the marvelous light that is your purpose.

If you had to remember one thing from all that you've read, remember this:

T.A.L.K.!

Keep going and acknowledge your divine help is always near! T.A.L.K. your way through your lowest valley! T.A.L.K. your way through your darkest hour! T.A.L.K., and you'll make it through!

LET'S T.A.L.K.: TRUST

Trust is not always an easy thing to do when you've been disappointed or betrayed. According to Oxford Languages (Oxford University Press, 2021), "trust" is both a noun and a verb. It means "firm belief in the reliability, truth, ability, or strength of someone or something" and "belief in the reliability, truth, ability, or strength of."

With that said, "what do you believe in God (or about God) regarding your situation?"

You know what you're going through, so be honest and truthful about your situation. This means being honest with yourself and with God. T.A.L.K. to God about what you're going through, and HE WILL SEE YOU THROUGH! God is greater than the problem you're struggling with.

You must also trust in the answer that God may give you because He knows you best. This is when you make sure you give it all to Him—all your grief, pain, worries (1 Pet 5:7)—and He will direct your path. God will provide whatever it is you need to get you through the problem. Just watch Him work everything out for your good (Rom 8:28).

During the final stages of an over 2-year Cosmetology program, I was falsely accused of cheating on a test and was in danger of being kicked out of school. After so many late hours and hard work, this would have been unbearable! Fortunately, God was with me, and due to my character (and God's grace), I didn't even have to defend myself. My teacher dismissed the allegation and advocated for me with the school's administration. God worked it out on my behalf! I don't even know what came of my accuser, but God rose up in my teacher and condemned the lying tongue.

When you're purposing to trust God, I believe you'll have to look inside yourself and tell Him all about your troubles. During the times when you may not have anyone physically present with whom to talk, know He is there, and you can tell Him anything. Still, it's important during those moments that you listen to His voice. He will let you know what you need to know at the right time. Just take time and listen to Him because He is your best friend and will never steer you wrong. He loves you and wants the best for you!

> *Casting all your care upon him; for he careth for you.*
>
> ‐   1 Peter 5:7 KJV

> *Trust in the Lord with all thine heart; and lean not unto thine own understanding. 6 In all thy ways acknowledge him, and he shall direct thy paths.*
>
> ‐   Proverbs 3:5-6 KJV

I think of the above scriptures because when I was struggling with my illness, I had to trust in the Lord and believe He was going to see me through my situation. Even when I shared my story with others, many people didn't believe me, and those that did could not understand that "the struggle was real." For example, as a proud military spouse, I found myself having to be mom and dad when my husband was away. It was hard for him to understand just how difficult normal, day-to-day tasks were for me. He may not have had a choice, but the military took him far away from home a lot, which made trusting him more difficult. Thankfully, his love for me caused a change and now our bond and trust are stronger than ever. He's shown unwavering support and even wrote the foreword for this book.

I understand and empathize if you're struggling with grief or illness, and you may not have the support (or, even, the compassion) from those around you. For me, and my hope is that it will be the same for you, I believed that God would deliver me out of all my problems. He knows more about me than I know about myself because He "knit me together in my mother's womb." God knew the words I needed to get out to let the people around me know I was telling the truth about what I was going through.

Yes, I was able to talk to God about what I was going through, and not only did He guard me, but He also gave me the very words I needed to say to those who would hear (and listen) to me. He gave me how to say what I needed to say. Finally, I experienced the peace of mind that someone heard me. That came from trusting God.

As I think about the depths of the pain of my first episode, I remember it as if it were yesterday. It was during the school week, and my eyes had been hurting for a few days. No one really took me seriously until I woke up one morning, and as I was getting ready to catch the bus to school. Shockingly, I couldn't see!

I don't know if you've ever experienced anything like this, but I was totally blind in my right eye. At that moment, I was terrified!

I believed God would give me the words to speak to whoever needed to hear me to help me. God saw me through it all like He always does. If I had to describe the pain I was feeling at that moment, it would have to be equivalent to someone reaching into my eye socket, pulling, and twisting my eyeball until it popped out! I remember it being a sharp, stabbing, unbearable pain.

Even when I took Tylenol®, the relief would not last long. It would allow me to sleep for short spurts, but I would soon feel the intensity of the pain again after taking each dose. It wasn't until the extensive testing over the next three weeks did my family and I receive the initial diagnosis from the neurologist that my world forever changed. This German medical professional told me that I had Multiple Sclerosis (MS). At the time, I couldn't even pronounce the words, let alone know what it was.

As you're reading this, you may be wondering what MS is. Well, according to the National Multiple Sclerosis Society, MS is an unpredictable disease of the central nervous system that disrupts the flow of information within the brain and between the brain and body. Further, in MS, damage to the myelin coating around the nerve fibers in the central nervous system (CNS) and to the nerve fibers themselves interferes with the transmission of nerve signals between the brain, spinal cord, and the rest of the body. Disrupted nerve signals cause the symptoms of MS, which vary from one person to another and over time for any given individual, depending on where and when the damage occurs.

The diagnosis of MS requires evidence of at least two areas of damage in the CNS, which have occurred at different times. Unfortunately, there are no cures but many treatments that may or may not work. A recent study reveals that nearly 1 million people in the U.S. are living with MS; each of us dealing with our share of pain.

I only share some of the aspects of the pain I've endured because it's important for you to know that I am God's child, and He is my Heavenly Father. Knowing that He sees everything I go through, knows everything I struggle with, and feels my pain! I believe He, sometimes, waits for me to just go to Him in prayer for what I need. He truly direct me through it all, and I thank Him all the time. He loves you just the same.

Trust is not easy for many people when they express the grief that accompanies the loss of a loved one or the pain that accompanies a chronic illness, but I believe you should pay close attention to the "T" in T.A.L.K.™ I've lived it, and God has seen me through it all. As a living testimony, I am sharing what I know will support you during some of your darkest and lowest moments.

What has gotten me through some of my toughest trials and tribulations can work to get you through yours. Therefore, I encourage you to TRUST God. I share this message with everyone because I believe everyone needs to trust God.

Have you ever had a friend who knew what you were going to say before you said it?

If you've had the privilege of having a friend like that, having God on your side is a thousand times better. He knows you like nobody else does. He knows you so well that the very hairs on your head are numbered (Luke 12:7). He knows how to usher you through your most difficult situations and circumstances. He will never steer you wrong!

HE WILL NEVER LEAVE YOU!

Be strong and of a good courage, fear not, nor be afraid of them: for the LORD thy God, he it is that doth go with thee; he will not fail thee, nor forsake thee. And the LORD, he it is that doth go before thee; he will be with thee, he will not fail thee, neither forsake thee: fear not, neither be dismayed.

- Deuteronomy 31:6, 8 KJV

Let your conversation be without covetousness; and be content with such things as ye have: for he hath said, I will never leave thee, nor forsake thee.

- Hebrews 13:5 KJV

Fear thou not; for I am with thee: be not dismayed; for I am thy God: I will strengthen thee; yea, I will help thee; yea, I will uphold thee with the right hand of my righteousness.

- Isaiah 41:10 KJV

Even if you do not believe in God right now, remember when you got out of that situation or circumstance and had no idea how? Know that it was God working it all out for you. He knows what's best for you, and He will guide you through it all!

I encourage you to trust in Him always!

I say "always" because you never know what will happen in a day or over the next week, month, and year. But God knows! He knows better than you or anyone else because He created us. We are "His workmanship," and He knows everything we're fraught with, so trusting God is essential to removing the frustration and doubt that may accompany our present condition.

I encourage you to trust in God through any and everything— whether you find yourself sitting in a restaurant or in your car driving home, TRUST God!

You may be asking, "Why should I trust God?"

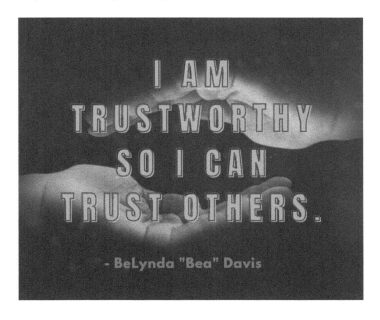

Or "What are the benefits of trusting God?"

My response is the same every time. Trust God because He knows all there is to know about you, and He will guide you in all things.

You may also be wondering, "How do I trust God?

Or "What do I need to do to trust God?"

To identify how you should trust in God, let me first remind you of that situation that someway, somehow, God got you passed that challenge. You learn to trust God by establishing a relationship with him and know that if He did it then, He can and will do it now.

I believe in these moments; God is talking to you, guiding you through the situation. You should practice trusting God because you need to have a relationship with Him. Trusting God makes that relationship grow stronger and stronger. As a result, you will not mind having a talk with God just like you would with a dear friend.

When you think of the "T" in T.A.L.K., know that it stands for "TRUST." I believe in having a conversation with God and being real. I found in doing that; I've always had something to say that expressing my deepest thoughts and pain becomes much easier to deal with.

Never be silent and never allow someone else to take your "voice!" Remember to talk and keep talking with Him (just like He's your best friend).

TRUST involves trusting in what you are saying to God and trust that He will lead you through it all.

No matter how often you talk to God, you must continue to keep doing so and never stop! Always say what you have to say because He knows the depths of your heart! He knows what you're trying to say even though you may not have the right words. Always keep the communication open.

If you feel comfortable, go to church! If you don't attend church, you can always go to the Bible. If you have a friend or somebody you know who has a personal relationship with God, you can go to that person or just go to God in prayer.

As you think of TRUST, I want to leave you with this, always talk to God, and He would not lead you wrong. Keep on trusting in Him because He knows all. He's waiting on you, so continue to always talk and trust, and He will make you victorious. Although it may not be when you want it, he is right on time. He will always be there for you when you need Him the most.

GOD WANTS WHAT'S BEST FOR YOU DURING YOUR TIME OF NEED SO TRUST!

LET'S T.A.L.K.:
TRUST REFLECTION QUESTIONS

Question #1: Do you think it is impossible to trust others? Why or why not?

_____

_____

_____

_____

_____

_____

_____

_____

_____

_____

_____

_____

Question #2: Do you believe people trust you? Why or why not?

_____

_____

_____

_____

_____

_____

_____

_____

_____

_____

_____

NOTES:
TRUST

LET'S T.A.L.K.:
ACCEPT

Have you ever had BIG dreams?

Have some of those BIG dreams been put on hold or stopped altogether?

Well, here's a funny quote, "If you want to make God laugh, tell Him your plans." This humorous statement touches on "ACCEPT," the next step of T.A.L.K.

From the time I was a young girl, I can remember wanting to be a cosmetologist. I loved the idea of making people look and feel beautiful! But, as my symptoms worsened, my battle with Multiple Sclerosis (MS) progressed. Thanks to God, I achieved my main goal of graduating from cosmetology school.

Due to my worsening conditions, some of my other goals had to change. It no longer includes doing hair and nails as I did before; however, I'm thankful that God's plan for me didn't end there because the best is yet to come! Yes, my ideas and other dreams being fulfilled seem uncertain at times, but my life is NOT over (and yours doesn't have to be either!)

There's so much going on now, but I've accepted that God has something better in store for me. I may not be able to run or work as I did before, but you're reading my published book, and I'm able to impact others by sharing my story. In other words, when one door closes, God opens another. I recall one of my early passions was running. As a young girl, I was one of the fastest on my track team, so they had me run the crucial anchor leg for our relay team.

I remember a particular track meet in Indiana. This day, for whatever reason, was unusually hot and humid. I don't remember why, but some of my fellow teammates did not make the meet. As a result, those of us there had to carry more of the load than expected. My coach was panicking as we didn't have our main participant in certain events. For the first time, I had to throw the shot put and, to my surprise, placed 2nd! I recall that day vividly due to the heat and the fact that I did something that I had never done before, not even in practice, yet performed very well. At this point, I began thinking to myself that I may have a future in athletics. Unfortunately, life had other plans.

Have you ever taken inventory of what you've accomplished already?

Are you grateful for the life you've been blessed to live each day?

If not, now's the time to reflect on your blessings and accept the beauty and joy of your present moment. I've learned to rejoice in my roles of wife and mother. When I became pregnant with my first child, DJ, I was very anxious. Over time, I saw it as a blessing and became joyful because, as a teenager, I was told that I might not be able to have children. Then, when BriAna arrived, I was doubly elated because God proved my doctors wrong and blessed me with two of the three loves of my life (the third being my husband, Steven, of course)!

Struggles with my health weren't the only thing I've had to overcome. Many mental and emotional challenges accompany physical illness. For me, I did not think a man would want to be with someone who could not bear any children. As previously mentioned, not only did God bless us with one child, but we have two healthy and beautiful children.

For those who may not be aware, military spouses are sometimes overlooked when it comes to the sacrifices we make to support our soldiers' careers. Don't misunderstand what I am saying. There's a lot of good from being a part of the military family, namely, free health care, a place to live, and a decent salary. However, with the late nights, early mornings, and frequent absences due to deployments and other "missions," the spouse is left raising the family on his or her own. Honestly speaking, I did not feel like I signed up for that.

This was because I grew up as a military brat. Although we moved periodically, my experiences as a dependent were drastically different from my experiences as a military spouse. Most military spouses end up making a support network that helps them cope with the hardships of military life. For example, a military spouse sometimes cannot have a career because they must find a new job every three to four years. Also, many soldiers often are unable to attend key family moments as part of the military life (e.g., births, graduations, etc.).

Although these issues are shared, most military spouses still could not understand what I was always dealing with. My illness made this situation even more challenging. Thankfully, God has always helped me take care of my household despite the added stress of being a military spouse!

If this doesn't prove God's plans supersede man's plans, I

don't know what does. After I accepted my circumstances, God manifested His plan for my life. Therefore, I encourage you to accept your present situation. When you do, you're able to find the peace necessary to receive whatever divine outcome is planned for your life. Sometimes, that makes all the difference in your healing.

Whether you're dealing with the loss of a loved one or a chronic illness, accept that your life is NOT over! God will help you through it all; just continue to have a talk with Him. When I first found out I had MS, it was devastating. The doctors gave me pamphlets and talked to me about the things I would have to deal with for the rest of my life. As I heard them talk, I said, "I'm not going to be able to do anything anymore." Knowing that there is not a cure for it, I thought my life was over. I really couldn't talk to anyone because no one could understand. I felt so alone. Going through MS, I had to take pills to ease the pain. I felt bad a lot of the day. I just wanted it to stop.

One day I was so tired of feeling the pain and having to take so many pills to get relief that I had a "serious" talk with God. I told him I was tired of taking pills and tired of people not understanding me. I asked God to have mercy on my soul because I wanted to die. I wrote a letter to tell everyone why I killed myself. I put it on my desk in my room. I said to God if I don't wake up, I know it was my time. If I do wake up, then it was not my time and that I just must deal with this MS. I didn't want to wake up, but God knew best. I said a prayer then, instead of taking one, I took four of my pain pills at bedtime. Surprisingly, I was at peace and I had the best sleep I had in an exceptionally long time.

The next morning came, and I woke up. I told God, I guess you have something more for me to do on this earth. I guess I'm going to have to deal with this forever. I took the letter off my desk, tore it up in pieces, and I said, here I go. God is my best friend, and since that darkest of moments, He's been guiding my footsteps. I believe He will also give you the instructions needed to make good things happen in your life. God has a plan and purpose for you; accept it, follow Him, and He will guide you in the way you need to proceed.

> *And lest I should be exalted above measure through the abundance of the revelations, there was given to me a thorn in the flesh, the messenger of Satan to buffet me, lest I should be exalted above measure. For this thing I besought the Lord thrice, that it might depart from me. And he said unto me, My grace is sufficient for thee: for my strength is made perfect in weakness. Most gladly therefore will I rather glory in my infirmities, that the power of Christ may rest upon me. Therefore, I take pleasure in infirmities, in reproaches, in necessities, in persecutions, in distresses for Christ's sake: for when I am weak, then am I strong.*
> -   2 Cor 12:7-10 KJV

It may not be easy to accept what God has placed before you, but know He did so with the intention of giving you grace sufficient for your challenge. He will not lead you wrong, and He always has your back (). God will lovingly guide you through the process of accepting your circumstances and your new journey.

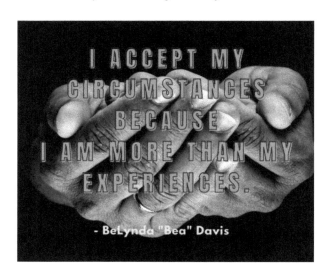

This acceptance was a major turning point in my journey of living with MS. I had to accept not being able to work in the salon any longer. I had to accept not becoming an Olympic athlete (at least I thought so). This became clear one day while I was cutting a client's hair. My hand started shaking and instead of cutting my client's hair, I was cutting my hand. I didn't notice it until I saw blood. I was cutting my fingers instead of my client's hair.

At that moment in 2004, I knew I would no longer be able to remain a cosmetologist. This would be my last time cutting hair. I knew I would not own my own salon and make many people look and feel good about themselves. I had to accept that, but I knew God still had other work for me to do!

I've continued to style hair occasionally, but "cutting hair" is out of the question for me, and that's OK. Anything more than a trim and style is a "no-go!" Still, I make people look and feel beautiful. It took some getting used to, but not doing hair professionally prompted me to transition to other things.

I was still able to do other things besides cutting hair to make women feel good while looking good. I remember talking to an older lady, who I could tell had not gotten her hair done in years. I talked to her and asked if I could do her hair. I told her she could just give me a donation for doing her hair. One day after she got off from work, she came to my house so I could do her hair. When I was done styling her hair, she looked at it and asked, "Is this my hair?" I said yes. She loved it and said thank you, thank you! She said she was going to the mall to show off her hair. Even her family came to me with great joy because they said I had changed their mom's life! I love making women feel good about themselves.

I can't do everything that I learned in school, but I can still do things in the cosmetology field. I went to a store one day. I said hi to someone with a smile, and she told me I had a beautiful smile. She said it made her day to see me smile. I told her, "That is awesome! This is the day that the Lord has made." She nodded in agreement. I still always talk about God. I will forever speak of His goodness. Like the song says, "He's done so much for me, I cannot tell it all." Having a talk with God helped me accept my new life.

If you've lost a loved one or friend or been diagnosed with an illness, and you've had to rediscover God's plan for you, God will steer you to where you need to go. God will lead you in knowing how you need to carry out His plan.

Even though you're unable to do some of the things you used to do, you can always talk to God about doing the work He wants you to do.

YOU HAVE A DIVINE PURPOSE, AND GOD WILL ENSURE YOU LIVE OUT YOUR PURPOSE!

T.A.L.K. to God about your problems, read your Word! T.A.L.K. to God often because having a conversation with God will assist you in developing the plan you need to move forward in your healing and faith.

I encourage you to stay positive and never be down on yourself. God will give you what you need to do and how you need to do it. Always lean on and depend on Him, and he will direct your paths (Proverb 3:5). Accept that there may be times when you have to cry.

LET IT OUT!

> *Weeping may endure for a night, but joy cometh in the morning.*
> - Psalms 30:5(b) KJV

God knows how to comfort you, and your joy will come! Let Him guide you in identifying your next move. Always keep talking and accept God's plan for your current situation. God will bless you so much that they will be too many to count!

If you didn't know, let me tell you right now...GOD HAS SOMETHING GREATER FOR YOU! This is not the last chapter of your life. Accepting this fact will accelerate the plan God has for you, and you will achieve more than you could ever imagine.

I declare…

GOD WILL USE YOU FOR HIS GLORY!

> ***And He said to me, "My grace is sufficient for you, for My strength is made perfect in weakness." Therefore most gladly I will rather boast in my infirmities, that the power of Christ may rest upon me.***
> *- 2 Corinthians 12:9 KJV*

LET'S T.A.L.K.:
ACCEPT REFLECTION QUESTIONS

Question #1: How difficult is it to accept your circumstances?

_____

_____

_____

_____

_____

_____

_____

_____

_____

_____

_____

Question #2: Can you accept the decisions you have made for yourself? Explain.

_____

_____

_____

_____

_____

_____

_____

_____

_____

_____

_____

_____

NOTES:
ACCEPT

LET'S T.A.L.K.: LOVE

What does "LOVE" mean to you?

The Oxford Learner's Dictionary (Oxford University Press, 2021) defines "love" as "a very strong feeling of liking and caring for somebody/something, especially a member of your family or a friend."

One of my favorite definitions of "love" comes from 1 Corinthians 13:1-13. The word "love" is written as "charity" in the King James Version of the Bible, but you'll get the point as you read below:

> *Though I speak with the tongues of men and of angels, and have not charity, I am become as sounding brass, or a tinkling cymbal.*
> *And though I have the gift of prophecy, and understand all mysteries, and all knowledge; and though I have all faith, so that I could remove mountains, and have not charity, I am nothing.*
> *And though I bestow all my goods to feed the poor, and though I give my body to be burned, and have not charity, it profiteth me nothing.*
> *Charity suffereth long, and is kind; charity envieth not; charity vaunteth not itself, is not puffed up,*
> *Doth not behave itself unseemly, seeketh not her own, is not easily provoked, thinketh no evil;*
> *Rejoiceth not in iniquity, but rejoiceth in the truth;*

Beareth all things, believeth all things, hopeth all things, endureth all things.

Charity never faileth: but whether there be prophecies, they shall fail; whether there be tongues, they shall cease; whether there be knowledge, it shall vanish away.

For we know in part, and we prophesy in part.

But when that which is perfect is come, then that which is in part shall be done away.

When I was a child, I spake as a child, I understood as a child, I thought as a child: but when I became a man, I put away childish things.

For now we see through a glass, darkly; but then face to face: now I know in part; but then shall I know even as also I am known.

And now abideth faith, hope, charity, these three; but the greatest of these is charity.

It's extremely important to KNOW WHAT LOVE IS and how much YOU ARE LOVED! What comes to mind is when I graduated high school in Germany. When I walked the stage to shake my principal's hand and receive my diploma, he told me I had many family and friends cheering for me. I said, "yes, I do." I felt so loved that day. Since I was in Germany, my blood family from the United States could not make it, but my church family stepped up and supported me. I felt a lot of love that day.

When you start from a place of love, you'll know that you are loved through all your trials and tribulations. One of my most challenging trials came from my husband's job. He was a black military officer, and because they are so few, he believed he had to be so much better than the other officers (who were not black). This made him work twice as hard and volunteer for the hardest assignments. Additionally, he deployed to combat zones and other areas I cannot mention in this book. This went on for years, and the impact on me was devastating. I cried to God often because I did not understand why he chose to do this job and leave me with our son knowing my condition. It was in these dark moments that I began to understand what love really is. It's not so much about getting my way or what I want, but it's about commitment and deciding to love for better or worse.

GOD LOVES YOU!

God is "love!" He knows what you need, so it's always great to talk to God. You'll forever have a listening ear and a shoulder to cry on. Whatever you say, don't worry; God knows your heart. He loves you. If you're feeling worried, sad, pain in your body, or frustration, know you are not alone, and He hears your every cry!

> *…put thou my tears into thy bottle: are they not in thy book?*
>
> - Psalms 56:8 KJV

GOD IS WITH YOU!

You never need to feel alone because He "sticks closer than a brother." (Proverbs 18:24 KJV); I find this scripture reassuring because it reminds me that I always have someone to talk to, even when my family and friends are unavailable. It does not matter what I've gone through;

God is always available to me. His availability is NOT only for me; it's also for YOU!

Knowing that God loves you and He is available should encourage you to give life one more day, give yourself one more chance, and give Him all the glory. If you've lost a loved one and are having a hard time, He is right beside you. He is the one whispering words of encouragement and every positive thought.

Some days, it may be extremely hard to get out of bed, go to the store, or visit with other family and friends. But He loves you beyond measure, sacrificing His Only Begotten Son for you. When you think you won't be able to make it another day, know that GOD IS WITH YOU! You're still here today, and this is proof of God's love for you!

When I think of GOD'S LOVE, I remember John 3:16:

> *For God so loved the world, that he gave his only begotten Son, that whosoever believeth in him should not perish, but have everlasting life.*
>
> - John 3:16 KJV

Because I Know God gave His only begotten son for us, I know He loves mankind; you and I included! When you take a moment to talk to Him, you will begin to know Him better. If you know a gospel song, or a gospel artist (like one of my favorites, Kirk Franklin), God's Spirit and power will fill you! You can listen to the words of a song and meditate on the love God has for you and the divine purpose for your pain, loss, or illness.

Forget about call-waiting or having to wait on a family member or friend, God is right there, and he is on time and never late!

One day in church, I can remember going to the altar to get prayer for my illness. I was told by a minister of the church that I was coming to the altar too much. My "instruction" continued as I was told to stop going to the altar because he said my constant coming to the altar showed a lack of faith, and I would not receive my healing. Talk about a gut punch! It was extremely hurtful since I was younger. It also prevented me from going to the altar for a while. I was shocked that someone in ministry would say that to someone in need of God's healing power.

Well, you need not worry about hearing that from me. I'm going to share something with you (something I didn't hear that day):
YOU CAN GO TO GOD'S ALTAR RIGHT WHERE YOU ARE AND AS MANY TIMES AS YOU WANT!

> *Then were there brought unto him little children, that he should put his hands on them, and pray: and the disciples rebuked them. 14 But Jesus said, Suffer little children, and forbid them not, to come unto me: for of such is the kingdom of heaven. 15 And he laid his hands on them, and departed thence.*
>
> -   Matt 19:13-15 KJV

You don't have to worry about how many times you go to "God's altar" because you are welcome in His "most-holy-of-holies!" As you go up there, God hears you. He wants you to talk to him. He wants you to release whatever you have built up inside of you so you can be free (John 8:36 KJV).

God's love is so deep; He'll be there for you no matter the situation or circumstance.

> *For I am persuaded, that neither death, nor life, nor angels, nor principalities, nor powers, nor things present, nor things to come, Nor height, nor depth, nor any other creature, shall be able to separate us from the love of God, which is in Christ Jesus our Lord.*
>
> - Romans 8:38-39 KJV

That's why I purpose to love the Lord with all my heart. I will always believe in Him. I want to share a story with you of when I was in the hospital during an episode with MS. This was a time that was unbearably hard for me. It was almost impossible for me to walk, and one of the nurses came up to me and said, "you probably will not ever walk for the rest of your life." She went on to say that it would happen to me soon. Recalling my battle with suicide, I remembered that God had a plan for my life, so I left the decision up to Him!

I believed in God for what he was going to do. I mention this story to encourage you to just say whatever is on your mind or your heart. That day, I had faith enough in God to disregard the words of someone who did not "knit me together in my mother's womb" or have my best interest at heart. I chose to have faith that it was not time for me to lose the use of my legs or be dependent on a walker at that time. You may also have people around you or run into people who believe they know your future, but I encourage you to talk with God about your outcome. He has the final say!

> *Come unto me, all ye that labour and are heavy laden, and I will give you rest.*
> - Matt 11:28 KJV

Many people will have an opinion about your life, but God is the author and finisher of your faith (Heb 12:2). When I experienced that situation with the nurse, I was 21 years old. It was not until almost two decades later that I needed a walker. Just think, if I had accepted the future the nurse was speaking over my life, I would not have walked into many wonderful situations over the years, like walking the stage to graduate Cosmetology school. Even now, I'm still feeling good, able to move around, and am choosing to live each day to the fullest!

If you are reading this, you are alive, and God is not finished with you yet. You have a purpose beyond your loss, your pain, and your illness. Even if you're only able to do some of the things you used to, keep moving forward with your dreams and the vision God gives you for your life.

If there is one key point about LOVE I'll share with you, it is this:

NO MATTER WHAT YOU GO
THROUGH,
NO MATTER WHAT ANYONE ELSE
BELIEVES ABOUT YOU AND YOUR
SITUATION, KNOW THAT GOD IS
WITH YOU AND LOVES YOU!

He is love, so don't take that for granted! Instead of listening to someone who is hindering you from feeling God's love, remember to talk to God and remember His LOVE for you is real!

If you can't look through scripture or sing a song, just talk to God. He is listening to you, and he loves you more than you can ever know. God will always be there; no matter the time of day it is, he is there! Just know…

…GOD IS LOVE!

HE IS ALWAYS WITH YOU!

HE IS IN EVERY SONG TO ENCOURAGE YOU!

HE KNOWS YOUR EVERY PAIN AND KNOWS THE

REASON FOR EVERY ONE OF YOUR TEARS!

God knows when and why you're crying out. In your pain, He is right there with you. In your sickness, He is right there with you. In your loss, He is right there with you. Despite your pain, He can be your comfort and peace when you "keep your mind stayed on Him (Is 26:3)!"

I encourage you to be true to yourself and whatever is going on, believe you can deal with whatever you're going through, and come out victorious. God's love for you will never fail! Just keep talking with God, and He will help you through it all!

Take a moment to reflect on your most challenging situation or circumstance. As you continue reading, there will be ample space for you to write down your definition of "love" and how God's love is revealed in your life. As you reflect, you may want to jot down any stories or scriptures you have, and you can read over them or write directly in the book. You will always have your notes to reflect on as often as you'd like since you'll have them with you. You should also go to the "word" (a.k.a. the Bible). You can meditate on what you've read and written down. You can go over them as many times as you need! When you remember to talk to God, His love for you will continue to be revealed to you. As you talk, you are speaking life over your situation and circumstance.

> *Death and life are in the power of the tongue: and they that love it shall eat the fruit thereof.*
>
> - Prov 18:21 KJV

Know that God's love is unending. Remember, He gave His Only-Begotten Son for you! He is there for you at any time. I remember an old saying about God's timeliness, "He may not come when you want him, but he's right on time!" Just lean and depend on God because He will never fail you. So, listen to what He speaks into your heart and mind and just T.A.L.K.

LET'S T.A.L.K.:
LOVE REFLECTION QUESTIONS

Question #1: Is it difficult for you to love yourself? Explain why or why not.

_____

_____

_____

_____

_____

_____

_____

_____

_____

_____

_____

Question #2: Is it challenging for you to show love to others? Explain why or why not.

_____

_____

_____

_____

_____

_____

_____

_____

_____

_____

_____

NOTES:
LOVE

LET'S T.A.L.K.: KNOW

Can you think of a time when you just knew that you knew something? I remember an old saying that says, "you have to know that you know that you know."

Well, that's what it means to "know!"

When you "know" something, little to nothing can change your mind.

In this step of T.A.L.K., we'll address "Know!" When you "know" something, you have knowledge obtained from your environment, your experiences, or from another outside source. There is also a spiritual aspect of "knowing," like when God has anointed you or revealed something to your spirit.

When you have this knowledge, there's isn't anything that you can't get through. When you KNOW the power of God within you, you're able to handle your most challenging situation or circumstance. Being a military spouse is incredibly challenging on its own, from the constant moving; to the having to make new friends; to the unfamiliar surroundings. It was comforting for me to KNOW that things would be better once we found a church family.

After Steven finished his basic officer course, our first duty location was Biggs Army Airfield in El Paso, Texas. DJ had a very scary accident that required a visit to the emergency room. As usual, my husband was on one of his "missions" and not in the country. I somewhat panicked because my son tried to put a hair bead on his ear to mimic an earring, but it went completely inside his ear. Once at the Army medical clinic, I was assured the medical personnel would take care of my son. Boy, was I wrong! They were all gathered around him like he was the subject of some experiment. It seemed to me that they were more interested in the story of what he did rather than helping. Instead, they made things so much worse that he had to have emergency surgery at a different hospital! Keep in mind; this was before GPS, so I had to find that other facility and we did not get to use the ambulance.

It was a Sunday morning, so I called my Pastor to let him know we would not make church service. Thanks be to God; he recognized the fear in my voice and met us at the other hospital. These are the kinds of incidents that come with the military lifestyle. It's a big deal having church family everywhere we've been. God works through others, and this was another fantastic example.

Just knowing that God will help you with your loss, your illness, or your grief is comforting, like having support from a good church family. The Lord is nigh unto them that are of a broken heart; and saveth such as be of a contrite spirit (Psalms 34:18 KJV). He is going to direct you in the way you should go. Always talk to Him about whatever you're going through, at any time and in any place.

If I have not said it enough times, God is there whenever you need Him. Dottie Peoples said it the best, "He's an on-time God, Yes He is." I understand there may be times when you don't feel like having a talk with God, or you may feel unworthy. It is in those times, you need to talk to God even more (and, perhaps, even longer!)! I can recall times when I didn't know what to say to God. But He gave me the words to speak back to Him. I would just pour my heart out because I felt like He was the only one who could understand me. Sometimes, it felt as if God was my only friend.

It may take some time, but KNOW He knows what you're going through. I thought of a time in my senior year in high school when the education board was going to pass a law that said you needed three years of a foreign language to graduate. I was incredibly nervous because I had not taken any language classes at all. I prayed to God, "Please do not let it be a reason I can't graduate." I said, God, you know what I need. Please, please, help me.

When the time came to tell us the results of what the board said, I was at my desk with my hands together, praying in my head. The person on the intercom said, "The education board decided to pass the law from the year 2000 and beyond. This meant I could still graduate without the special language classes. I was overjoyed! God knew what I needed. That might not be a big thing to some, but that was a huge mountain for me. I KNOW God and what He will do when we talk to Him.

If you don't feel good enough to talk to a family member or a friend, remember God is there all the time waiting patiently! He'll never say anything bad about you or lead you astray. Matthew 7:7 says, "Ask, and it shall be given you; …." Just know that God hears all! KNOW that whatever you must deal with, God will help you bear it (think Footprints in the Sand by Carolyn Carty, Flora Haines Loughead). He knows you're grieving, in pain, sad, or feeling lost. He knows you may be looking for someone to be right there beside you!

GOD KNOWS…

…and it's time you KNOW HOW MUCH GOD IS FOR YOU!

> *If God be for you, who can be against you.*
> -   Romans 8:31 KJV

God is there even though you may have infirmities and illnesses. Sometimes, you may feel like you cannot do anything! It's in those times you must remember that although you may not be able to do what you used to do, you're still here! It may take you longer, but you can still do it, and that's ENOUGH!

If you've survived a loved one, or you feel helpless to achieve your goals, it's in those times you're given the divine strength to keep going. Philippians 4:13 says, "I can do all things through Christ which strengtheneth me."

This reminds me of when I started an online medical coding program. My teacher was great and helped me every time I asked, which was all the time (it's ok to laugh here). I had to wait for her to get on the computer site I was on. We would be on one problem for an hour. It was like that for every assignment. She recommended I do another program. She said I would be good in the medical record specialist program. Both programs cost the same.

After I moved to the other program, I understood that class much better. I asked God to please let me pass with a high B. I really wanted an A, but I didn't think I could. Yes, it can be difficult, but I know God strengthens me to do all things. Therefore, I know exactly how it feels to be discouraged. When I finished the class, I made a B, but I was one point from an A. I took that as God saying that you should ask for what you want because you KNOW He can make it happen.

God will give you the strength to do what you need to and must do. KNOW God will give you someone you can talk to, even if He's the only one. He may also provide a group of people or a church leader who can be a "listening ear" or "shoulder to cry on."

KNOW YOU'RE NEVER ALONE!
God is there with you 24-hours each day. You've read to this point, so I believe you understand the importance of being able to T.A.L.K. your way to healing and recovery. When you talk about the uncertainties of an illness or life's circumstances and situations, we know this is the opposite of knowing. Therefore, with this step of T.A.L.K., the key point is to KNOW that you can eliminate uncertainty through the faith you have in God!

Ask God questions for understanding. Read scriptures to remind you of divine truth. Reference scriptures while relating the principles to your life or present situation, and read the testimonies of others to encourage you during your times of hardship. For example, my testimony may serve as encouragement for you during times of difficulty because of my battle with Multiple Sclerosis and life as a military spouse. Through it all, I KNOW GOD HAS NEVER LEFT MY SIDE!

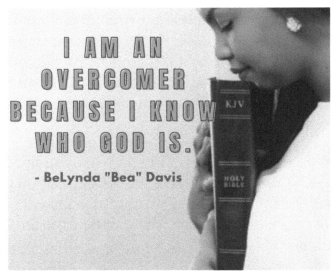

I AM AN OVERCOMER BECAUSE I KNOW WHO GOD IS.

- BeLynda "Bea" Davis

I KNOW walking will never be the same for me and that's ok. There is always the possibility of needing a wheelchair or using a walker when I need one. I KNOW I am still here and able to do exactly enough for each day. When my husband was gone because of the military, I had to be there for my children. It was particularly challenging, but we were able to get through it, which let me KNOW that God had not given up on us. He has given me the tools, resources, and family to help me get through everything. This goes for you as well because God will give you the help you need to make it through your grief, pain, and illness. They'll be a list of resources at the end that may help you as well.

Morning routines are especially helpful for me. When I get up every morning, I always tell God, "THANK YOU!" I always give thanks for waking me up. I encourage myself by saying, "Alright now, come on now!" and God helps me through it! It may take me a little longer to get going, but I know God is right there with me. That's why I start each day acknowledging that He's going to direct my path for the day.

I knew God had my back during one of my episodes with MS. I was looking around as usual, and everything started spinning. Everything around me was turning in circles, and it was as if I was riding a merry-go-round on the playground, going around and around. It seemed as if someone just kept spinning the merry-go-round and would never stop.

This truly scared me.

I didn't understand what was going on. Explaining this to someone who did not experience it was extremely difficult. I had to say, "God, please help me. I need your help!" Now, even when I was frightened the most, God still calmed me down. He let me know that He was with me through it all. I believe I heard Him say, "this too shall pass!" I knew my pain would not last forever, and I was able to go to my doctor and explain what was going on. God was my provider, *Jehovah Jireh,* because He provided "a peace that surpasses all understanding" and a calmness that I needed at that time. This peace and calmness can also be yours when you KNOW God is with you…always!

> *For I know the thoughts that I think toward you, saith the LORD, thoughts of peace, and not of evil, to give you an expected end.*
> - Jeremiah 29:11 KJV

> *And the peace of God, which passeth all understanding, shall keep your hearts and*

Let's T.A.L.K.

minds through Christ Jesus.

- Philippians 4: 7 KJV

The biggest takeaway I'd like to share with you is for you to KNOW that God is with you and KNOW that HE IS GOD! He has gotten you to this point and will not leave or forsake you. YOU CAN ALWAYS TALK TO GOD AND T.A.L.K. YOUR WAY TO LIVING YOUR BEST LIFE NOW!

God will be there for you whenever you need Him. KNOW that he loves you and wants the best for you. KNOW that when your situation or circumstance feels like you can no longer bear it, God will give you strength! He loves you that much and will take care of your every need.

When your lost loved one is no longer there to give that special word or phrase that you're used to hearing to help you in your situation, you may start to cry. It's in those moments you must KNOW God is listening. It's okay to cry. You may remember your loved ones because they are still "in your heart." When you have an illness that reduces your ability to do things like you're used to doing, God is there to help and guide you.

KNOW THAT EVERYTHING IS GOING TO WORK OUT FOR YOUR GOOD!

Your life will be the best that you can make it with God's help. God wants the best for you and will never leave you nor forsake you. KNOW He has your back and will provide whatever you need. He is there for you to get you past what you are going through; just KNOW you can talk to God about whatever it is. God provides strength, peace, and comfort during your most difficult trials and tribulations!

When you need more information about getting beyond your grief or uncertainty, talk to God about your situation, you can also meditate on the word of truth through the scriptures. You can even go to someone you trust, a Pastor or First Lady, and talk to them as well.

You can talk to them about what you're going through since the loss of your loved one or after an unexpected medical diagnosis. You may also be able to talk to your family members about your feelings of grief or uncertainty. Family members or friends who knew your loved one may be able to offer comfort as they recall memories that bring you joy.

Even when you're home alone or late at night when no one is available, God is there! As I've been saying throughout this book, KNOW God is with you and that you're able to talk to Him (at any time)! Whether you're having a talk with a pastor or a friend or just with God, always talk about what you're going through because that will help you turn your tragedy into triumph.

T.A.L.K. TO GOD!

LET'S T.A.L.K.:
KNOW REFLECTION QUESTIONS

Question #1: Read Genesis 1:26 below and answer the reflection question that follows.

And God said, Let us make man in our image, after our likeness: and let them have dominion over the fish of the sea, and over the fowl of the air, and over the cattle, and over all the earth, and over every creeping thing that creepeth upon the earth.

Do you know you are made in God's image? Explain how and/or why?

_____

_____

_____

_____

_____

_____

_____

_____

_____

_____

_____

Let's T.A.L.K.

Question #2: How does knowing God enable you to live joyfully and reach your destiny?

_____

_____

_____

_____

_____

_____

_____

_____

_____

_____

_____

NOTES:
KNOW

LET'S T.A.L.K.: YOUR ACTION PLAN

Congratulations!!!

You've reached the end of "Let's T.A.L.K: Your 4-Step Guide To Getting Beyond The Pain Of Loss & The Uncertainty Of Illness So You Can Live Your Best Life Now." Still, your journey to overcoming is beginning now!

You may be wondering, how do I live my best life now when right now, I don't think I can make it another day. Well, it starts with you deciding that you will not allow your current circumstances to dictate the outcome.

Additionally, what I mean by living your best life NOW is a walk of faith. That's why I took you on my journey so you could see how I could've given up. I didn't because my faith in God's plan and purpose for my life was found in my pain. I'm passionate about helping others realize that He will do it for them just like He did it for me. So, your best life is when you've found your purpose, your passion and are moving toward your destiny.

Remember, nothing is accomplished without work! Furthermore, the Bible says that faith without works is dead (James 2:20 KJV).

You've been introduced to T.A.L.K. and how it helped me on my journey. I've shared some of my losses and my wins to encourage you to understand that "with God, all things are possible." It is my prayer that you've gained insight from T.A.L.K., acknowledge that you are "more than a conqueror," and will write your own stories of defeating your challenges.

I also hope you willingly share your story of how you have been able to T.A.L.K. your way to your best life!

> *But Jesus beheld them, and said unto them, "With men this is impossible; but with God all things are possible.*
> - Matthew 19:26 KJV

> *Nay, in all these things we are more than conquerors through him that loved us.*
> - Roman 8:37 KJV

Below, you'll find your ACTION PLAN! As soon as you wake up, give thanks for another day. When you are getting ready for your day, look in the mirror and say each affirmation. Repeat the affirmations as many times as you need to. If you encounter daunting situations or challenging circumstances throughout your day, recite the affirmations.

You can also read and recite the companion scriptures, as they often gave me encouragement during my toughest times.

STEPS TO YOUR ACTION PLAN

1. Read each step of T.A.L.K.
2. Read and memorize each affirmation.
3. Read and meditate on each scripture as it applies to you.
4. Review your answers to the reflection question(s) for each step of T.A.L.K. and identify how you're using each step of T.A.L.K. in your life.

STEP 1: T = TRUST

Affirmation:

I AM TRUSTWORTHY, SO I CAN TRUST OTHERS.

Scripture:

Trust in the LORD with all thine heart, and lean not unto thine own understanding.
-    Proverbs 3:5 KJV

Though he slay me, yet will I trust him;….
-    Job 13:15

STEP 2: A = ACCEPT

Affirmation:

I ACCEPT MY CIRCUMSTANCES BECAUSE I AM MORE THAN MY EXPERIENCES.

The Serenity Prayer:

God grant me the serenity to ACCEPT things I cannot change, the courage to change the things I can, and the wisdom to know the difference.

STEP 3: L = LOVE

Affirmation:

MY VALUE IS IMMEASURABLE BECAUSE OF GOD'S LOVE.

Scripture:

> *For God so loved the world, that he gave his only begotten son, that whosoever believeth in him should not perish, but have everlasting life.*
>
> - John 3:16 KJV

STEP 4: K = KNOW

Affirmation:

I AM AN OVERCOMER BECAUSE I KNOW WHO GOD IS

Scripture:

> *In all thy ways acknowledge him, and he shall direct thy paths.*
>
> - Proverbs 3:6 KJV

Ultimately, you want to T.A.L.K. to yourself to overcome your daily challenges so you can live your best life NOW! As you use the T.A.L.K. method, take a moment to review your responses to the reflection questions. As time goes by, you should see progress in how you respond to each one. It's important to know that your growth and healing processes will take some time. But, looking back to see how far you've come will encourage you to keep moving forward!

NOTES:
YOUR ACTION PLAN

_____

_____

_____

_____

_____

_____

_____

_____

_____

_____

_____

RESOURCES & SUPPORT

FOR MILITARY SPOUSES
Association of Military Spouse Entrepreneurs
https://www.amse.co/

FOR MULTIPLE SCLEROSIS
MS Society -
https://www.naitonalmssociety.org/
Can Do Multiple Sclerosis Support Group –
https://www.cando-ms.org/
Multiple Sclerosis Association of America –
https://mymsaa.org/
myMSteam –
https://mymsteam.com/

FOR SUICIDE
National Suicide Prevention Lifeline -
1(800)273-8255
https://suicidepreventionlifeline.org/
American Foundation For Suicide Prevention -
https://afsp.org/

FOR GRIEF
Grief Share -
https://www.griefshare.org/
Grieving.com -
https://forums.grieving.com/
Grief Anonymous [Best social media group for 2021 (FB)] -
http://www.onlinegriefsupport.com/groups
Online Grief Support (Best specific grief 2021) -

http://www.onlinegriefsupport.com/groups

TEXT LINES & OTHER SUPPORT SERVICES
Crisis Text Line – Text 741741
(Trained counselors servicing the United States)
Grief Text Line – Text 839863
Or Call 1(800)445-4808
SAMHSA National Helpline
1-800-662-HELP (4357)

RESOURCES & SUPPORT SERVICES YOU

WOULD LIKE TO LIST:

_____
_____
_____
_____
_____
_____
_____
_____
_____
_____
_____

ABOUT THE AUTHOR

Woman of God, committed wife, and loving mother are just a few phrases that describe **BeLynda Davis**. Affectionately called "Bea" by her family and friends, Mrs. Davis is a virtuous woman from humble beginnings who decided over 2 decades ago to stand in the face of adversity. She is a walking testimony to the faithfulness of God and His divine support.

Born in Madisonville, Kentucky, Mrs. Davis spent most of her formative years as an "Army Brat" which allowed her to travel to places like Hawaii and Germany. Her family moved every few years to a different military base, so she learned to be flexible and adapt to her environment from an early age. It was not until her 10th grade year of high school when she was shocked with an all new (and unexpected) reality. Mrs. Davis was diagnosed with Multiple Sclerosis (MS) and her life would be forever changed.

Mrs. Davis found solace in attending church and, after joining the choir, soon discovered her gift of singing. She's also accomplished her childhood dream of "making people look and feel beautiful" by graduating from Ogeechee Technical College (Statesboro, GA) where she received her degree in Cosmetology. Mrs. Davis also received her Medical Records Specialist Certification in 2016.

Now, God has called Mrs. Davis to transition from working with her hands to working with her words! "Let's T.A.L.K.: Your 4-Step Guide To Getting Beyond The Pain Of Loss & The Uncertainty Of Illness So You Can Live Your Best Life Now" is Mrs. Davis' first published book and it speaks to the hearts and minds of individuals who have lost a loved one or are struggling with a chronic illness! She's on a mission to share her story with the world and encourage others to T.A.L.K. their way through hardship. Mrs. Davis has been featured in the media and on various podcasts.

She is a supportive military spouse. Mrs. Davis navigates the daily challenges of strengthening her marriage, growing her family, and supporting her husband, Steven, who has been on multiple combat deployments. As she continues to conquer everything that comes her way, Mrs. Davis happily resides in Illinois with her loving husband and darling children, DJ and BriAna! For more information, visit http://inspired2inspire.co/ or email admin@inspired2inspire.co.

SPECIAL NOTE:

ADDITIONAL BOOKS, PRODUCTS, & SERVICES COMING SOON!

For up-to-date information & VIP updates, visit
http://inspired2inspire.co/

Also, please LIKE & SHARE our Facebook Business

page by visiting
https://www.facebook.com/inspired2inspirellc

NOTES:
ADDITIONAL NOTES

_____
_____
_____
_____
_____
_____
_____
_____
_____
_____
_____

NOTES:
ADDITIONAL NOTES

CPSIA information can be obtained
at www.ICGtesting.com
Printed in the USA
BVHW060108160721
612045BV00023B/861